Best Egg Recipes

Published by Blue Dome Press
535 Fifth Avenue, Ste. 601
New York, NY 10017-8019, USA

www.bluedomepress.com

Art Director Engin Çiftçi
Graphic Design Veysel Demirel
Photographs Semih Ural

ISBN: 978-1-935295-53-2

Printed by
Imak Ofset, Istanbul - Turkey

Best Egg Recipes

*From the Ottomans
to the Contemporary Turkish Cuisine*

M. Ömür Akkor

BLUE DOME

New York

Contents

Preface

Good Day!

Eggs are used in Turkish cuisine as a supplement in a great many desserts and dishes. However, in traditional Turkish cuisine eggs are not only used in a wide variety desserts and dishes, but they are even served as desserts and main dishes themselves. In old Turkish cookbooks, one could find a section entitled "Egg Dishes," but in contemporary Turkish cookbooks, such a chapter is nowhere be found. We would never like those special dishes to be lost, and this is why we have prepared an anthology of egg recipes.

God bless those who prepare them and bon appetite to those who taste them!

M. Ömür Akkor

Why Eggs?

In order to have an adequate and balanced diet for leading a healthy life we should never omit eggs from our meals, as eggs are both affordable and have great nutritious value.

- Starting from the sixth month on, eggs are a valuable source of nutrition for children. If a child's intake of iron is poor, that child will likely develop anemia. Moreover, iron plays a role in growth, development and protection from diseases.

- Lack of protein in a pregnant woman's diet may cause low birth weight for her baby, which may lead to such chronic diseases later on as diabetes, obesity, high blood pressure, etc. A single egg eaten once a day will help satisfy the needs of a pregnant woman regarding protein intake and help ensure a healthy birth weight.

- Choline, a nutrient found in eggs, plays a significant role in children's brain development.

- It is recommended that men get 550 mg of choline and women 425 mg daily to maintain health.[1] (A large hardboiled egg contains 113 mg of choline; to compare, 5 ounces (142 g) of raw beef liver contain 473 mg, and 15 grams of soy lecithin granules contain 450 mg).[2]

- During pregnancy, the need for choline increases 7 times over.

---

[1] "Choline: An Essential Nutrient for Public Health," http://www.ncbi.nlm.nih.gov/pmc/articles/PMC2782876/

[2] "Choline," http://en.wikipedia.org/wiki/Choline

- When eggs are eaten regularly, they are scientifically proven to protect from cancer and cardiovascular diseases, maintain and protect the health of the digestive system, relieve symptoms of menopause, and prevent osteoporosis.

- Young girls who regularly consume eggs have a decreased risk of breast cancer later in life.

- Consuming eggs decreases the risk of stroke.

- Eggs protect the health of the eyes and decrease the risk of visual disorders and cataracts later in life.

- When cooked appropriately, eggs are a low calorie food despite their high nutrient profile.

- With thirteen different nutrients (including high-quality protein, choline, riboflavin and vitamin B12), eggs are the easiest, the most delicious, and the cheapest way to eat healthy.[3]

Chicken egg (whole, hard-boiled)
Nutritional value per 100 g (3½ oz)

Energy	647 kJ (155 kcal)
Carbohydrates	1.12 g
Fat	10.6 g
Protein	12.6 g
Water	75 g
Vitamin A equiv.	149 µg
Thiamine (vit. B1)	0.066 mg
Riboflavin (vit. B2)	0.5 mg
Pantothenic acid (B5)	1.4 mg
Folate (vit. B9)	44 µg
Vitamin B12	1.11 µg
Choline	294 mg

---

[3] "All About Eggs," http://www.thenibble.com/reviews/main/cheese/eggs/egg-nutrition.asp

Vitamin D	87 IU
Vitamin E	1.03 mg
Calcium	50 mg
Iron	1.2 mg
Magnesium	10 mg
Phosphorus	172 mg
Potassium	126 mg
Zinc	1.0 mg
Cholesterol	424 mg

(For edible portion only. Refuse: 12% (shell). One large egg is 50 grams).[4]

In a Nutshell

- There is no other food as delicious, as nourishing, and as affordable as the egg.
- Eggs are not processed and do not need to be, due to their natural packaging.
- The nutrients found in eggs, the most important of which is choline, directly affect brain development and help in raising smart and successful children. Choline is a nutrient component which should be taken in as part of one's diet as it cannot be manufactured in the body.

---

[4] "Egg (food)," http://en.wikipedia.org/wiki/Egg_(food)

Eggs in Ottoman Cuisine

In this section, we share with you some information in order to help you understand eggs and their place in Ottoman cuisine. Generally, in modern day Turkish cookbooks, there are no separate headings for eggs, but their importance is unquestionable, for they constitute the basis of many foods.

Dishes to which eggs are added: Much of Ottoman cuisine used to be prepared with eggs. It is known that for fifteen centuries, eggs have been added to *tarhana*, (a traditional Turkish cereal consisting of flour, yoghurt, and vegetables which are fermented and then dried; it is consumed as a soup by mixing it with stock or water), *börek* (a flaky pastry typically filled with thin layers of cheese or ground beef), *kalya* (vegetables fried in oil), fried eggplants, lamb dishes, *lalanga* (a pancake-like dessert eaten with syrup or sugar), a dish cooked with leeks, and *pide* (a round flat bread, similar to pita). Soups and stews were seasoned with eggs due to their binding qualities as well as being used for milk desserts, and pie and dough fillings.

The etymology of the Turkish word for egg: The word *yumurta* was derived from roots of the words of *yumru* and *yumruk,* which mean "rounded" and "in the shape of a ball or fist." As for the word *lop* in the phrase *lop yumurta*, which means a hard-boiled egg, it was borrowed from the French "*lobe*," meaning soft and circular objects. Historically, instead of the word *omlet*, which is borrowed from French (*omelette*), the words *gaygana* or *kaygana* were used in Turkish.

Kaygana (Turkish omelet): It used to be cooked with sugar, jam, minced meat, eggplant or parsley. Mustafa Ali, from Gelibolu (1541–1600), who was a poet, writer and historian, recorded that *kaygana* was a very flexible recipe.

Honey *kaygana*: Kaygusuz Abdal, a 15th century Ottoman poet, mentions "honey *kaygana*." In the recipes of the same century, *kaygana* was cooked as a thin layer of dough which was soaked in water and dipped into beaten eggs. Afterwards, the *kaygana* were laid down, one on top of another, and fried in oil. From the eighteenth century onward, this method of cooking has been abandoned.

Seller of Eggs, Istanbul, 1904.

Fried patty with beaten eggs: In the treatise of Ali Ashraf Dede, the recipe for the patty goes as follows: "Into a mixture of egg *kaygana* there should be added bread crumbs and then put into a saucepan (where the vegetable patty is cooked). It should be cooked in the shape of a patty, after which honey sherbet is added."

Egg whites: Egg whites were used not only in many desserts, especially those which included sugar, but also in almond cookies, *halwa kahi* (a kind of *beze*, or meringue), and in creamy *baklava* (finely layered pastry filled with nuts and steeped in syrup). In the first Ottoman cookbook, entitled *Maljau't-Tabbahin* (The Shelter of Cooks), there are a great many sherbet recipes where egg whites are used. Hans Dernschwam, a German traveler, reported that on his visit to İstanbul in 1553, he was very fond of a dessert made with almonds, egg whites and honey.

The spoon used to eat soft boiled eggs: A special spoon is mentioned in the Ottoman books regarding the officially fixed prices in 1640. The spoon, which was a unit of measurement, was probably used to eat soft boiled eggs.

Significance of eggs in the period of Sultan Mehmed the Conqueror: Eggs used to be bought for the Ottoman Palace in large amounts and were used in the preparation of a large variety of foods, from porridges to *börek* pastry. It was also recorded that duck eggs were cooked especially for Sultan Mehmed the Conqueror.

Egg porridge: This kind of meal was prepared with an abundant amount of eggs, garlic, and yoghurt. One can come across this kind of recipe in kitchen records of the period of Sultan Mehmed the Conqueror.

***Enderun* egg (eggs prepared with onions):** Eggs cooked with onions by Ottoman chefs for the Sultan were quite famous. The secret of this food, which especially astonished foreign visitors with its extraordinary taste, was that it was based on frying thinly sliced onions in a large quantity of oil for a long time. In exams organized to test the progression of cooks professionally, it was required to prepare onions with eggs for the Sultan.

Red eggs: During Easter, Ottoman citizens with Roman, Armenian, and Syrian backgrounds used to dye hard boiled eggs a red color.

***Beyza*:** This word was used historically instead of *yumurta*, as determined by Süheyl Ünver in his research done on foods eaten in the period of Sultan

A woman from Karaman, from the
album of Lambert de Vos, 1574.

Mehmed the Conqueror. The word *beyzi,* from a similar root, also means "oval, in the shape of an egg."

Eggplant roast: A kind of eggplant dish cooked with meat, eggs, and yoghurt, served in the palace of the Ottoman Sultan in the 15th and 16th centuries.

Hard boiled eggs sold in markets: In his treatise written in the year 1545, Luigi Bassano, an Italian traveler, described in detail everyday life of the Kanuni (Suleiman the Magnificent) period. Among the readymade foods sold at markets, there were hard boiled eggs sold in pairs.

Fresh eggs: In the book *The Housewife,* published in 1915, Ayşe Fahriye Hanım stated the following: "The most light, delightful and delicious of eggs is a fresh chicken egg. Cooking it for a long time will take time and spoil the stomach; (hence) it should be prepared quickly. As the yolk of an egg is much more nutritious than the egg white, it is definitely healthier than the latter. Eggs can be preserved by being buried in straw, cinder and bran. The purpose here is to prevent moisture in the air from spoiling the egg. If the egg is covered with extinguished lime, then it would be preserved even better."

Fish soup with eggs: In *Maljau't-Tabbahin*, there is a recipe for a soup that is prepared by adding 50 egg yolks to 1.3 kg of sea bass (1884).

Egg sauce: The Italian word *salsa* was transmitted into Turkish as *salça* and was formerly used as the name for sauces. Here is a recipe Ayşe Fahriye Hanım gives in her 1915 cookbook regarding egg sauces: "Take fifteen *dirham*s[5] of flour of good quality, the same amount of butter, 150 *dirham*s of half boiled hot water and salty meat broth. Whip 2 egg yolks adequately and add 5 *dirham*s of butter. Strain it through a colander. Add some parsley. This sauce is used for grilled game meat and fish."

***Durr al-Maknun*(Hidden Pearls):** In this treatise written by Yazıcıoğlu Ahmed Bican (d. 1466), eggs are recommended as a remedy for fragile, slender and pale faced people.

Egg delight: In the dessert booklet *At-Tarkibat fi Tabhi'l-Hulwiyyat,* written in the 19th Century, which was translated into contemporary Turkish in part

---

[5] 1 *dirham* is approximately 3 grams.

through the zeal of Günay Kut, one can find the following recipe of egg delight: "Put 9 egg whites and corn starch into a bowl. Whisk them till bubbles appear. Put the mixture into boiling oil with a spoon. Take out when they get puffy and golden. Then, pour some melted sugar or honey on them."

Börek **made with eggs:** This famous food was prepared in the kitchen of the palace for Sultan Mehmed the Conqueror and his surrounding people on the third of Shawwal (the tenth month of the Arabic calendar), in 1474.

Narcissus salad: This kind of egg salad, known in Siirt, is called "narcissus salad" because it resembles white and yellow narcissus.

Ottoman Cookbooks

Ottoman Cuisine of the 15ᵗʰ Century **by Muhammad bin Mahmud Shirvani:** Shirvani, an Ottoman doctor, wrote the first distinct recipe book of the Ottoman period. Egg recipes given in his book include *Mutancana*[6] with Egg, Fried Eggs, and *Güllaç*[7] with Egg.

Maljau't-Tabbahin **(The Shelter of Cooks) by Mehmet Kamil:** This book bears the honor of being the first Ottoman cookbook ever published, written by one of the teachers of the Imperial Medical School and published in 1844. This book contains many egg recipes for dishes such as soups, stews, *pilaki* (a stew of dried beans or fish with olive oil and onions, eaten cold), meatballs, *börek*, stuffed vegetables, many desserts recipes, bean patty, vegetable patty (the chief ingredient of which is squash), and eggplant patty recipes, eggplant *kaygana*, Turkish delight with eggs, and poached eggs made with yoghurt.

Turkish Cookery Book **by Turabi Efendi:** Mehmed Said Pasha, the Ottoman governor of Egypt, visited England, and organized a dinner for the statesmen in 1862. There, the cookbook *Maljau't-Tabbahin*, translated by Turabi Efendi under the name *Turkish Cookery Book*, was handed to guests that visited the banquet. Turabi Efendi did not only translate this book, which was published in England in 1864, but also made some changes in it, increasing the number of chapters and adding other recipes. His work was

---

[6] Cube lamb cooked with julienne cut dried figs, apricots, pearl onion and fresh onion.

[7] Rice wafers stuffed with nuts.

the only source of Turkish cuisine in the Western world for many years. The book includes recipes for Ordinary *Kaygana*, Ground Meat *Kaygana*, Egg-plant *Kaygana*, Dessert *Kaygana*, Parsley *Kaygana*, Jam *Kaygana*, Poached Eggs, and Turkish Delight with Eggs.

A Food Treatise of Ali Ashraf Dede: This treatise was written by Ali Ashraf Dede, one of the heads of Edirne Mawlawi Dervish lodge, in 1858 and was edited and republished in 1992 by Feyzi Halıcı. In this book, there were recipes for egg based foods such as Egg *Kaygana* Patty, Eggplant Patty, and Eggplant *Kaygana* and Meatballs.

The Chief Cook by **Mahmud Nedim bin Tosun:** The author of this book, written in 1898, was in fact a soldier. After his assignment to the town of Bulanık of Muş, he missed the home cooked meals his mother made and wrote this book for those of his soldiers who had no one to cook for them. Recipes mentioned in the book include Poached Eggs with Yoghurt, Spinach Eggs with Herbs, Tomato Eggs, Sausage or Cured Spiced Beef with Eggs, Ground Meat Eggs, Cheese Omelet, Onions with Eggs (*Mıhlama*), Soft Boiled Eggs, Egg Salad, Rice with Eggs, and Curd Balls with Eggs.

The Housewife by **Ayşe Fahriye Hanım:** This treatise, published in 1915 and one of the most significant Turkish cookbooks, includes the following egg dishes: Egg Sauce, Mushrooms with Eggs, *İşkembe* (Tripe) with Eggs, Sausage with Eggs, Ground Beef with Eggs, Cured Spicy Beef with Eggs, Onions with Eggs, Soft Boiled Eggs, Spinach Eggs, Dill Eggs, Hard Boiled Eggs, Artichoke Eggs, Butter Eggs, Eggs with Olive Oil, Cheese Eggs, Eggs with Cream, and Chickpeas with Eggs.

Fabulous Cookery Book by **Vağinag Pürad:** Vağinag Pürad was a traveler on the famous transatlantic *Titanic* and miraculously survived the tragic accident during the ship's maiden voyage. He wrote a book of Turkish recipes entitled *Fabulous Cookery Book*; included in his cookbook are recipes for Egg Sauce, Soft Boiled Eggs, Meat Broth with Eggs, *Shakshouka* (a dish made with peppers, onions, and eggs), Nuts with Eggs, Eggs with Cream, Kidney with Eggs, Mushrooms with Eggs, Eggs with Tomato Paste, Artichoke with Eggs, Liver with Eggs, Poached Eggs, Egg *Kaygana*, Simple Omelet, Green Pea Omelet, Poached Eggs in Tomato Sauce, *Mucur* (a kind of omelet), Bean *Mucur*, Eggplant *Mucur*, and Sauce and Tomato *Mucur*.

MEASUREMENT TABLE

1 cup water or milk	250 ml / 8 oz
1 cup granulated sugar or rice	200 g / 7 oz
1 cup flour	140 g / 5 oz
1 tablespoon granulated sugar	15 g / 0.5 oz
1 tablespoon butter	15 g / 0.5 oz
1 tablespoon tomato or paprika paste	15 g / 0.5 oz
1 tablespoon flour	15 g / 0.5 oz
1 tablespoon olive oil	15 ml / 0.5 oz
1 teaspoon salt	6 g / 0.2 oz
1 teaspoon black or red pepper	3 g / 0.1 oz

Cheese Rissoles with Eggs

Of all the forgotten egg recipes, this is one of the healthiest and most delicious—we cannot forget to include it. I strongly recommend you try this recipe taken from the Mahmud Nedim bin Tosun's unique book *The Chief Cook*. If you wish, you may cook these fantastic curd rolls, often used as appetizers, in the oven. They could also be served between 2 slices of bread. They are the best and healthiest snack food for children. Though Mahmud Nedim bin Tosun wrote that this dish would be truly amazing if prepared with uncured curds from the islands of İstanköy and Midilli, it is quite apparent that preparing this dish with homemade Bursa curds will make it one of a kind. If you can't get your hands on fresh homemade Turkish cheese and don't feel like making any yourself, you can use store bought cheese labeled "farmer's" or "pot cheese," or try to find Russian style *tvorog* or German *käse quark*.

Ingredients

4 eggs

1 pound fresh farmer's or pot cheese

2 tablespoons chopped scallion

2 tablespoons chopped dill

4 tablespoons chopped parsley

2 tablespoons flour

1 teaspoon salt

½ teaspoon black pepper

4 tablespoons oil

Preparation

Break 2 eggs into a medium bowl. Add fresh cheese, chopped herbs, flour, salt and black pepper. Mix them well for 2 minutes. Beat the other 2 eggs in another bowl. Pour the oil into a medium saucepan over medium high heat. Shape walnut sized balls of the cheese mixture, press them lightly to make rissoles, dip them in the beaten egg, and deep fry till crispy both sides (for about two minutes). Place fried cheese rissoles on paper towel to soak up excessive oil. Place the cheese rissoles on a plate, and serve.

Serves 4 to 6.

Mıkla

ℰ✦

This is one of the egg dishes from the period of Sultan Mehmed the Conqueror known as "Egg Mash" or *Mıkla*. This meal can be served hot as well as cold. It is just as delicious eaten as a cold leftover as it is warm and freshly prepared.

Ingredients
1 pound (condensed) yoghurt
1 mashed garlic clove
1 teaspoon salt
1/3 cup olive oil
6 eggs
½ teaspoon black pepper

Preparation
Put the yoghurt, garlic, and salt into a medium bowl. Beat the mixture for a few minutes. Pour the olive oil into a medium pan and break eggs directly into the same pan. Place the pan on the stove and heat over a medium flame, stirring occasionally and slowly scrambling the eggs. Once cooked, turn off the heat and set the pan aside to cool for 5 minutes. Add them to yoghurt along with oil. Sprinkle with black pepper, and serve warm or cold.

Serves 4 to 6.

Poached Egg

This recipe is closely related to *mıkla*, a kind of fried egg. I have adapted this recipe from *The Chief Cook* written by Mahmud Nedim bin Tosun. Let's have a look at a recipe for poached eggs from the past.

Ingredients

4 cups water

1 teaspoon salt

4 tablespoons vinegar

4 eggs

1 mashed garlic clove

½ pound yoghurt

2 tablespoons butter

1 teaspoon red pepper flakes

Preparation

Place a medium pot with water on the stove, add the salt into it, and heat over a medium flame. Add the vinegar as soon as water starts to boil, and lower the heat. Break the eggs one by one into the boiling water very carefully without breaking the yolks. Let them boil for a few minutes. While eggs are boiling, smash the garlic with the salt and add it to the yoghurt, mixing thoroughly. Put the boiled eggs onto a deep plate using a slotted spoon and pour the yoghurt over the eggs. In a small saucepan, melt the butter and mix the red pepper flakes in it. Pour this sauce over the eggs and yoghurt, and the dish is ready to serve.

Serves 4.

Onions with Eggs

This was one of the meals from the period of Sultan Mehmed the Conqueror and was the favorite food of Ottoman Sultans. Nowadays, we make a simplified version of Onions with Eggs, but in the past some recipes called for it to be cooked for 3 hours. Another interesting fact is that during Ottoman times, it was thought that if a cook prepared this dish well, then all his other meals would be delicious. I would like to share with you the most sublime egg dish of the Ottoman cuisine, right from the imperial table to your kitchen.

Ingredients

3 medium white onions

3 tablespoons butter

¼ cup water

1 tablespoon vinegar

1 teaspoon brown sugar

½ teaspoon allspice

4 eggs

½ teaspoon black pepper

½ teaspoon cinnamon

1 teaspoon salt

Preparation

After peeling off the outer skin, leave the onions whole and slice them across the layers, making circle-shaped slices. Salt the slices. After 10 minutes, rinse them. Melt the butter in a medium pan over medium low heat, and as soon as butter is melted add the onion slices and sauté them for 10 minutes. Add the water and continue to cook, covered, over low heat for about 1 hour. Then add the vinegar, sugar, and allspice. Break eggs over the sautéed onions and cover; cook for 5 minutes more till eggs are cooked through. Sprinkle with black pepper, cinnamon, and salt, and serve.

Serves 4.

Honey Bites

This is a fantastic recipe for an Ottoman egg dessert. I truly enjoy the taste of this dish, which I adapted from *The Chief Cook*. I would recommend eating it at an evening meal or at tea time.

Ingredients

4 pieces of stale bagels

3 eggs

1 cup oil for frying

6 tablespoons honey

1 tablespoon sesame seeds

Preparation

Crumble the stale bagels in a medium bowl (or make them flour in a blender). Break the eggs into the same bowl, mix them into the crumbs, and knead the mixture into dough. Shape the dough into walnut sized balls. Heat approximately 1 cup of oil over high heat and fry the balls till they become golden, for about 3 minutes. Put on a plate and pour honey over them. Sprinkle sesame seeds, and serve.

Serves 4 to 6.

Tomato *Mucur*

❧

Here is a fantastic recipe for you from the *Fabulous Cookery Book*. You can use up your stale bread and cook a delicious meal. I have transcribed here a version of *mucur* made with tomatoes; you can make the simple recipe given here, or add sausage or beans if you wish.

Ingredients

2 medium tomatoes

20 fresh mint leaves

4 slices of stale bread, broken into crumbs

4 eggs

1 teaspoon salt

½ teaspoon black pepper

6 tablespoons olive oil

1 tablespoon sweet red pepper paste

20 thinly sliced garlic cloves

Preparation

Peel the tomatoes, remove the seeds, dice them in small cubes, and put them in a medium mixing bowl. Grind the stale bread, and break 4 eggs into the bowl. Add finely chopped mint leaves, salt and black pepper. Mix them well for 2 minutes. Heat 4 tablespoons olive oil in a large pan over medium high heat, and fry the mixture for 8 minutes, till crispy both sides. Put the remaining olive oil with garlic and sweet red pepper paste in a small saucepan, fry for 1 minute and turn off the heat. Slice the tomato *mucur* on a cutting board, put them on a serving plate, pour the sauce over them, and serve hot.

Serves 4.

Eggplant with Eggs

During Ottoman times, this dish was prepared by first boiling and then frying eggplants. But we have made a small change, and instead of boiling and then frying eggplants, we have used roasted eggplant. This simplifies the recipe a bit.

Ingredients

2 whole eggplants (medium-sized and roasted)

1 tablespoon butter

1 tablespoon pine kernels

1 tablespoon dried currants

1 tablespoon salt

2 eggs

½ teaspoon black pepper (or parsley for garnish)

Preparation

Finely chop roasted eggplants. Then, melt the butter in a medium pan, and fry the pine kernels over medium heat. After frying for a few minutes, add currants, roasted eggplants, and salt. Continue frying them all together, stirring the pan and ensuring the mixture heats through.

When the eggplants, currants and pine nuts are quite hot, break the eggs over the mixture. Cook the eggs to your preferred doneness, scrambling them or leaving them to poach in the eggplant mixture, and serve garnished with black pepper or parsley.

Serves 2.

Egg Bites

I wanted to share a recipe for Egg Bites taken from the first Turkish cookbook *Maljau't-Tabbahin* (*The Shelter of Cooks*), written by Mehmet Kamil. This fantastic cookbook was published in 1844 and has since become a bestseller; it has been printed 9 times, and is a very important source of recipes for us in Turkey. Tonight, you may prepare this delightful dessert.

Ingredients

2 cups water and 2 cups sugar for the syrup

1 cup flour

¼ tablespoon salt

½ cup water

3 eggs

1 cup oil for frying

¼ pound cream

1 tablespoon ground pistachio nuts

½ tablespoon cinnamon

Preparation

Put the water and sugar in a medium pan over medium heat, and boil for 5 minutes. Turn off the heat and set the pan aside to cool for 1 hour. Mix flour, salt and water in a medium pan until it forms dough, and cook it over medium low heat, stirring constantly while it cooks. As soon as the mixture hardens, remove the pan from the heat. Set aside to cool for 10 minutes. When the mixture has cooled enough to be comfortable to the touch, break the eggs into it and mix well. Heat oil in a large frying pan over medium heat, and measure the dough by spoonful into the hot oil and fry. Place the fried pieces of dough in the syrup for 10 minutes. Place the desert on a serving dish and decorate it with cream, pistachio nuts, and a sprinkle of cinnamon.

Serves 4.

Jam *Kaygana*

❦

Though we usually cook savory omelets, Ottoman cuisine presents a great variety of jam and honey omelets. Here is one of the fantastic jam *kaygana*s found in Ottoman cuisine.

Ingredients

4 eggs

1 tablespoon flour

¼ cup milk

1 tablespoon butter

4 tablespoons raspberry jam or your favorite jam

1 tablespoon confectioner's sugar

Preparation

Break eggs into a medium mixing bowl, beating thoroughly. Add the flour and milk, and mix well. Melt butter in a large frying pan till it sizzles, and pour the egg mixture into the pan. Cook for 3 minutes on one side and then flip over to cook the other side. After it is done, place it on a large flat plate and put the jam in the center. Fold it in half, making a half moon shape, and then fold it in half again; sprinkle with confectioner's sugar and it is ready to be served.

Serves 2.

Garbanzo Beans with Eggs

❧

This is one of the most important recipes of the Ottomans, which can be cooked with or without meat; you may also add more herbs if you wish.

Ingredients

1 tablespoon butter

¼ pound finely chopped lamb

½ teaspoon salt

½ medium onion (chopped)

½ cup boiled garbanzo beans

3 eggs

½ teaspoon red pepper flakes

Preparation

Melt the butter in a medium frying pan and add the lamb; after a few minutes add the salt and onion.

Fry the meat and onion over low heat for about 30 minutes. Then add the garbanzo beans and eggs (as whole). When eggs are done according to your favor, take dish off the heat. Season with salt, sprinkle with red pepper flakes, and serve.

Serves 2.

Çiğ Köfte with Eggs

This is a main dish that I learned of while spending time in Şanlıurfa. I was entranced by this dish and didn't eat anything else during my time in Şanlıurfa but this; the taste of *çiğ köfte* (chee kufta) with eggs was simply unbelievable. Though the recipe I give here uses butter, you may make this dish with clarified butter if it's available to you.

Ingredients

1 medium tomato

1 cup finely ground cracked wheat (bulgur)

1 tablespoon paprika paste

1 teaspoon salt

2 tablespoons red or chili pepper flakes

1 medium onion (chopped)

4 tablespoons thinly sliced parsley

4 tablespoons thinly sliced scallion

3 tablespoons butter

5 eggs

Preparation

Peel the skin off the tomato and dice them in small cubes. Place raw bulgur in a large tray. Add tomatoes, paprika paste, salt, and red pepper flakes. Fill a cup with water and keep it next to you. Wet your hands and begin kneading the mixture together, occasionally wetting your hands as you knead. After kneading for 15 minutes, add onion, parsley, and scallion. Continue kneading for a few minutes more. Then rest the dough for 10 minutes.

Meanwhile, melt the butter in a medium frying pan over medium high heat. Fry the eggs sunny side up (or over easy, to your taste). Pour the cooked eggs with their butter onto the dough you previously made. Mix the eggs and dough together with a spoon, put on a serving plate, and serve hot.

Serves 4 to 6.

Mantı (Turkish Ravioli) with Eggs

One piece of this *mantı*, or Turkish ravioli, is almost 1 portion. You may make this dish even more delicious by adding sage leaves, chamomile, or similar fresh herbs to water intended for boiling. One more point—do not forget to pour some olive oil on *mantı* before serving.

Ingredients

Dough:	Filling:
1½ cups flour	½ pound spinach
2 eggs	½ pound soft, uncured cheese
1 tablespoon olive oil	8 eggs
¼ cup water	1 teaspoon salt
	4 teaspoons extra-virgin olive oil
	½ teaspoon black pepper

Preparation

Put all ingredients needed for dough in a large bowl and knead together to form a smooth, hard dough—about 5 minutes. Cover the dough with a wet cloth and rest it for 20 minutes. Meanwhile, fry spinach in a large pan for a few minutes, until it wilts. Take off the heat, add soft, uncured cheese (farmer's or pot cheese) and mix. Crack the eggs, separating the yolks from the whites, taking care to keep each yolk whole, and set both aside. Divide dough into 2 lumps and roll them out.

Cut the rolled dough into squares, 2 inches by 2 inches (5 cm by 5 cm), and place a spoon of the spinach mixture into the center of each square. Spread spinach almost to edges of each square, making a space in the center. Place an egg yolk in the space. Repeat for all 8 dough squares. Brush the edges of dough squares with 1 egg white. When finished, cover the square with another one. Cut 8 egg ravioli with knife into squares.

Fill a pot with 2 cups of water, add salt and bring to a boil. When water starts to bubble, add ravioli and boil for 4 minutes. When they are done, remove the ravioli and place on a serving plate or individual dishes. Drizzle with extra-virgin olive oil, sprinkle with salt and black pepper and serve. If you wish to, you may add sage or other fresh herbs to the cooking water for a tantalizing aroma while the ravioli cook.

Serves 2 to 4.

Spinach with Eggs

"Spinach with Eggs" is a dish cooked by everyone and is one of the most important egg dishes in Turkish cuisine. I give you here a recipe for cooking it with onions, but if you wish you may make it with minced meat in addition to the onions. You can even add leftover rice!

Ingredients

1 medium onion (chopped)

1 tablespoon butter

1 teaspoon salt

½ teaspoon black pepper

1 pound fresh diced spinach

4 eggs

Preparation

Preheat the oven to 170°C (338°F).

Fry the onion in a large pan with the butter. Add salt and pepper. After frying for 5 minutes, add spinach and fry for 5 minutes more. Place the spinach and onions into a casserole dish, break the eggs over them. Bake for 15 minutes, and serve.

Serves 4.

Rice *Kaygana*

There is a great variety of ways *kaygana* are prepared in the different regions of Anatolia, including sweet, savory, and vegetable *kaygana*. This is a fantastic *kaygana* recipe that can be made with leftover rice.

Ingredients

10 romaine lettuce leaves

3 tablespoons chopped scallion

1 tablespoon chopped parsley

1 tablespoon chopped fresh mint

½ pound cooked rice (leftover rice is perfect)

4 eggs

1 tablespoon flour

1 teaspoon salt

½ teaspoon black pepper

1 cup oil for frying

Preparation

Put the romaine lettuce leaves, scallion, parsley, and mint in a medium mixing bowl. Add rice, eggs, flour, salt, and black pepper, and mix together thoroughly. Heat the oil in a large frying pan, and fry the *kaygana* mixture by spoonful, one by one. Deep fry till crispy both sides, and put them on some paper towels to draw out the excess oil. When all of the batter is cooked, put the *kaygana* on a plate, and serve. You may also add hot pepper sauce if you wish.

Serves 4 to 6.

Egg Salad

This salad is no longer as commonly prepared in Turkey as it once was, but it is quite delicious and is particularly good served for breakfast. If you wish, you may serve it with small rolls.

Ingredients

4 hardboiled eggs

2 medium peeled tomatoes

¼ pound farmer's cheese

4 tablespoons chopped parsley

4 tablespoons chopped scallion

Juice of 1 lemon

3 tablespoons extra-virgin olive oil

1 teaspoon salt

1 teaspoon red pepper flakes

Preparation

Dice eggs, tomato, and farmer's cheese in small cubes. Put them into a medium bowl. Add parsley, scallion, lemon juice, olive oil, salt and red pepper flakes. Mix carefully without smashing the egg. Place the salad on a plate, and serve.

Serves 4.

Stuffed Eggs

This is a fabulous recipe for an egg dish from the city of Bursa. While writing a book on cuisine in Bursa, I inquired about this dish; it is a meal that is known by everyone, but which has been almost completely abandoned to the past. I have prepared a recipe with a filling made of herbs for you. If you wish, you may make the filling with minced meat or cheese.

Ingredients

7 eggs

1 tablespoon chopped scallion

2 tablespoons chopped parsley

2 tablespoons flour

½ teaspoon black pepper

½ teaspoon red pepper flakes

½ teaspoon salt

1 cup oil for frying

Preparation

Boil the eggs for 12 minutes. Shell the hardboiled eggs and cut them in half lengthwise. Remove the yolks and put them in a bowl. Add to the yolks the scallion, parsley, black pepper, red pepper flakes, and salt. Knead the mixture together well. Make yolk-sized balls and put these back into the egg white halves.

Beat the remaining egg in a bowl. Roll the stuffed egg halves in flour and then dip them into the beaten egg. Heat oil in a medium frying pan and fry the stuffed halves over medium heat. Place egg halves on a napkin or cloth to remove excess oil as you fry them, and then serve.

Serves 4.

Egg Pizza
with Spinach

❧

This is not only a very delicious egg dish, but it is also very convenient. Moreover, your children will love this pizza very much.

Instead of spinach, you may use other greens or herbs, as well as varying the type of cheese.

Ingredients

½ pound chopped spinach

½ cup white cheese (*feta*)

½ cup *kashar* cheese

4 eggs

½ teaspoon salt

½ teaspoon black pepper

2 pieces *lavash* bread

Preparation

Preheat the oven to 200° (392°F).

Put the spinach, white and *kashar* cheese in a large bowl. Break in 2 of the eggs, add the salt and black pepper, and mix them.

After putting the bread on a baking tray, spread the mixture on them, leaving an empty space in the center of the bread. Break the remaining 2 eggs over the spaces. Bake for 10 minutes, and serve.

Serves 2.

Ground Beef with Eggs in an Earthenware Cooking Pot

Today I'd like to give you a well-known recipe for ground beef with eggs that is prepared in an earthenware cooking pot. Preparing it in a cooking pot and then baking it in the oven greatly increases its taste. And, if the eggs are cooked in individual dishes, it will look as amazing as it tastes.

Ingredients
½ medium onion

2 medium tomatoes

1 green pepper

1 red pepper

1 tablespoon butter

½ pound ground beef

1 teaspoon salt

½ teaspoon black pepper

4 small earthenware cooking pots

4 eggs

Preparation
Preheat the oven to 200°C (400°F).

Finely dice the onion, tomato, and green and red pepper. Melt the butter in a medium pan over medium heat and fry the onion for a few minutes. Add peppers and ground beef, fry 5 minutes more. Add the diced tomato, and fry all ingredients for a few minutes. Add salt and black pepper. Remove from the stove and divide the prepared mixture equally into the small cooking pots. Break 1 egg into each of those pots and bake in the oven for about 15 minutes, and serve. (You may bake the eggs for more or less time, according to your own taste.)

Serves 4.

Egg Puffs

This is made with egg whites. You may make it plain, as given here, as well as with dried fruits or nuts added to the whipped egg whites.

Ingredients

2 cups granulated sugar

4 egg whites

2 drops lemon juice

A pinch salt

Preparation

Preheat oven to 100 to 110°C (225°F).

Using a hand mixer and a large heatproof bowl, whip the granulated sugar and egg whites with the lemon juice and a pinch of salt for a few minutes. Then, put the bowl over a low flame and whip for 10 minutes more. Take the bowl off the heat and continue beating for 10 minutes more. When the mixture does not fall off the beaters and becomes stiff, it means that the mixture is ready.

Spread parchment paper out on a baking tray. Put the mixture on the parchment paper with a spoon, or fill a cake decorator with the egg white mixture and pipe onto the parchment paper, making small rounds.

Bake puffs in oven until they become dry but before they brown, approximately 8 minutes, and serve.

Serves 4 to 6.

Potatoes with Eggs

This is a classic egg dish, mainly prepared by university students in Turkey. If you wish, you may add cheese, tomatoes, peppers or anything else that you have in the kitchen.

Ingredients

2 medium potatoes

4 eggs

1 teaspoon salt

1 cup oil for frying

½ teaspoon thyme

Preparation

Peel potatoes, wash and dice them in small cubes. Deep fry till golden and put aside. Break eggs in a mixing bowl, add salt, and beat. Put potatoes in a medium pan and spread them out evenly. Pour beaten eggs over the potatoes and cook over medium heat. When eggs are done to your liking, you may sprinkle thyme on them, and serve.

Serves 2.

Menemen

Everyone in Turkey knows what *menemen* is. Some eat it without pepper, others without onions, but classic *menemen* cannot do without pepper and onions.

Ingredients

2 red peppers

½ medium onion

3 medium tomatoes

2 tablespoons butter

4 eggs

1 teaspoon salt

½ teaspoon black pepper

Preparation

Finely dice red peppers and onions. Peel the tomatoes and dice in small cubes. Melt butter in a medium pan and fry onions over medium heat for a few minutes. Add red peppers and tomatoes. Fry together 5 minutes, and then break eggs into the pan. Scramble the eggs gently into the vegetables. Continue cooking until the eggs are cooked to your liking. Sprinkle with salt and black pepper, and serve.

Serves 4.

Fried Egg with Artichoke

❧

Artichoke and eggs are both important sources of nutrients for our health; this recipe makes use of both, and should be tried, as it is delicious. Make sure to add the lemon juice, for lemon gives it a completely unique, delicious flavo

Ingredients

2 boiled artichoke hearts

2 tablespoons olive oil

½ teaspoon salt

2 eggs

1 tablespoon chopped dill

½ lemon

Preparation

Mash the artichoke hearts in a large bowl with a fork, or with a mortar and pestle. Heat the olive oil in a medium frying pan over medium heat and add the mashed artichoke hearts and salt. Fry them for about 3 minutes. Break the eggs over the hearts and cook the eggs to your liking, scrambling or frying it as you prefer. Mince the dill, sprinkle it over the egg and artichoke hearts, squeeze the lemon, and serve.

Serves 2.

Pastrami with Eggs

This is everyone's favorite egg dish. I recommend
that you prepare and serve it this way.

Ingredients
4 small ramekins
½ tablespoon melted butter
8 slices *pastrami* without cumin
4 eggs

Preparation
Preheat the oven to 180°C (350°F).

Grease the ramekins well with butter. Put the *pastrami* in the
ramekins, making the shape of a cross on the bottom.

Bake the ramekins in the oven for 10 minutes. Take them out of
the oven and separate the eggs, placing 1 yolk and half of the
white in the center of the ramekin. Bake till eggs are done to
your liking, and serve.

Serves 2 to 4.

Herb Omelet

Though there are many varieties of omelets, the one with plenty of fresh herbs is the best.

Ingredients

4 eggs

1 tablespoon flour

¼ cup milk

2 tablespoons chopped parsley

2 tablespoons chopped fresh mint

¼ pound grated *kashar* cheese

½ teaspoon salt

¼ teaspoon black pepper

1 tablespoon butter

Preparation

Break eggs into a large mixing bowl. Add flour and milk and whisk well. Add parsley, mint, cheese, salt, and black pepper, and whisk again. Melt the butter in a medium pan over medium heat, and then pour the omelet mixture into the pan.

Lower the heat and fry both sides; alternately, you may cover the pan and cook the omelet as it is in the pan, without flipping it, and serve.

Serves 2.

Deviled Eggs with Mustard, Turkish Style

This egg dish is prepared differently today than it used to be; the recipe I give below is a more modern version. The method given below is fairly simple; however, you may add anything to the filling mixture, according to your desire.

You may decorate these fantastic stuffed eggs with herbs as well as use them in salads. Be as creative as you like with them.

Ingredients

6 eggs

1 tablespoon mustard

1 tablespoon mayonnaise

½ teaspoon salt

A few dill leaves

½ teaspoon powdered red pepper

Preparation

Boil the eggs for 12 minutes. Once cool, shell and halve them. Take out the hardened yolks and put them in a medium mixing bowl. Add the mustard, mayonnaise, and salt. Mix them well until they become a smooth paste.

Put this filling back into the egg white halves using a spoon or cake decorator. Garnish the stuffed eggs with dill and red pepper, and serve.

Serves 4.

Egg Salad with Tuna Fish

❧

This is indeed a different recipe. While we often use eggs only for breakfast dishes, this dish makes use of eggs as part of a delicious luncheon meal. The flavors of the fish and capers meld wonderfully, cultivating a superb taste I suggest you try soon.

Ingredients
6 eggs
½ pound canned tuna fish
2 tablespoons olive oil
4 tablespoons capers
½ lemon
3 tablespoons mayonnaise
½ teaspoon salt
½ teaspoon black pepper

Preparation
Hard boil the eggs for 12 minutes. When eggs are finished, let them cool slightly, shell them, and cut them in half lengthwise. Arrange eggs on a serving plate according to your desire.

Strain tuna well and put it into blender. Put tuna fish, olive oil, 2 tablespoons capers, and lemon juice in a blender and blend until they become a smooth paste. Put the paste in a medium mixing bowl, add mayonnaise, salt and black pepper, and blend again with a mixer. Pour the sauce over the eggs. Sprinkle with the remaining capers, and serve.

Serves 4 to 6.

Asparagus with Eggs

Though it would seem that the use of asparagus in Turkish cuisine is European in origin, it is actually widely used in Anatolian and Aegean cuisines.

Asparagus can be fried in olive oil with stale bread, or cooked in a large pan with onions and eggs; in Anatolia, asparagus is cooked with olive oil, lemon juice, or in a flaky pastry. Today, I would like to give you a recipe for a simple but very delicious meal with asparagus and eggs.

Ingredients

8 asparagus spears

4 eggs

1 tablespoon flour

¼ cup milk

½ teaspoon salt

½ tablespoon butter

Preparation

Boil asparagus in a pot full of water for 10 minutes, and then strain them in a colander. Break the eggs into a medium mixing bowl. Add flour, milk and salt and whisk together.

Melt the butter in a large frying pan over medium heat, and pour the beaten eggs into the pan, cooking until the eggs are set; then flip the omelet and cook the other side. Put the omelet on a cutting board, lay the boiled asparagus lengthwise on the omelet and roll them up in it. Slice the roll, arrange slices on a plate, and serve.

Serves 2.

Cheese Soufflé
with Eggs

Cook this dish right away. The taste of it will be unforgettable. It is especially well suited for breakfasts and tea times.

Ingredients
4 eggs
1¼ cup milk
½ pound grated white cheese
½ teaspoon salt
½ teaspoon black pepper
2 tablespoons butter
8 slices sandwich loaf

Preparation
Preheat oven to 190°C (375°F).

Break eggs into a medium mixing bowl. Add milk, cheese, salt and black pepper and beat together. Grease a small casserole dish with butter. Spread the remaining butter onto the bread slices.

Place 4 slices of sandwich loaf on bottom of the casserole dish. Pour half of the egg mixture over them. Layer the rest of the bread over the eggs, and pour the rest of the egg mixture over all. Bake for 20 minutes, and serve.

Serves 4.

Creamy Mushrooms
with Eggs

A delicious dish from world cuisine ... It is a perfect option
for breakfast or brunch.

Ingredients

15 medium-sized fresh mushrooms

4 eggs

1 tablespoon butter

½ teaspoon salt

½ teaspoon black pepper

1 tablespoon chopped parsley

4 tablespoons of cream

Preparation

Preheat the oven to 200°C (400°F).

Wash and cut the mushrooms into thin slices. Finely chop the
parsley. Separate the egg whites and yolks. Melt the butter in a large
pan over medium heat and sauté the mushrooms for 5 minutes.
Add the salt, black pepper, parsley, and cream. After adding the egg
whites, mix them well for 2 minutes. Divide the prepared mixture
equally into 4 small cooking pots. Put an egg yolk on top of each pot.
Bake them for about 10 minutes, and serve.

Serves 4.

Salmon and Caviar
Hors D'oeuvres

Not only main dishes or desserts use eggs – these delicious hors d'oeuvres also use them. In the recipe, I have used salmon and caviar, but you may vary the toppings according to your desire.

Ingredients

4 eggs

3 tablespoons cream cheese

2 tablespoons chopped dill

10 slices of bread or 10 crunchy, salted crackers (Saltines, for example)

3 tablespoons mayonnaise

2 oz. black caviar

2 oz. smoked salmon

Preparation

Boil eggs for 12 minutes. Meanwhile, mix cream cheese and 1 tablespoon dill in a small bowl. Spread the mixture on 5 slices of bread or crackers, and put mayonnaise on the remaining 5 pieces. Take eggs out of boiling water, let them cool until comfortable to the touch, and then shell them and slice them in circles.

Place a piece of egg on each slice of bread or cracker. Evenly divide caviar between 5 hors d'oeuvres, placing the caviar on top of the egg slice. Evenly divide smoked salmon between remaining hors d'oeuvres, in the same manner as the caviar. Sprinkle the remaining dill over eggs, and serve.

Serves 4.

References

And, Metin, 1994, *16. Yüzyılda İstanbul: Kent, Saray, Günlük Yaşam* (İstanbul in the 16th Century: Town, Palace and Daily Life), İstanbul: Akbank.

Ayşe Fahriye Hanım, 1915, *Ev Kadını* (The Housewife), İstanbul: Arif Efendi Publishing House.

Halıcı, Fevzi, 1992, *Ali Eşref Dede'nin Yemek Risalesi* (A Food Treatise of Ali Ashraf Dede), Ankara: Atatürk Kültür Merkezi.

Işın, Princilla Mary, 2010, *Osmanlı Mutfak Sözlüğü* (Ottoman Dictionary of Culinary Words), İstanbul: Kitap.

Kut, Günay, 1986, *At-Tarkibat fi Tabhi'l-Hulwiyyat: Tatlı Pişirme Tarifleri* (Dessert Recipes), Ankara: Kültür ve Turizm Bakanlığı.

Mahmud Nedim bin Tosun, 1998, *Aşçıbaşı* (The Chief Cook), edited by Princilla Mary Işın, İstanbul: Yapı Kredi.

Mahmud Shirvani, 2005, *15. Yüzyıl Osmanlı Mutfağı* (Ottoman Cuisine of the 15th Century), edited by Mustafa Argunşah, Müjgan Çakır, İstanbul: Gökkubbe.

Mehmet Kamil, 1997, *Maljau't-Tabbahin* (The Shelter of Cooks), translated by Günay Kut, Turgut Kut and Cüneyt Kut, İstanbul: Unipro.

Pürad, Vağinag, 1926, *Mükemmel Yemek Kitabı* (Fabulous Cookery Book), İstanbul: Takvor Mardirosyan Publishing House, translated by Takuhi Tovmasyan, 2010, İstanbul: Aras.

Şavkay, Tuğrul, 2000, *Osmanlı Mutfağı* (The Ottoman Cuisine). İstanbul: Şekerbank-Radikal.

Toygar, Kamil, 1998, *Türk Mutfak Kültürü Üzerine Araştırmalar* (Researches on the Culture of Turkish Cuisine) Ankara: Türk Halk Kültürünü Araştırma ve Tanıtma Vakfı.

Turabi Efendi, 2005, *Osmanlı Mutfağı* (Turkish Cookery Book), translated by Altay İltan Aktürk, İstanbul: Dönence.

Ünver, Süheyl, 1952, *Fatih Devri Yemekleri* (Dishes of the Period of Sultan Mehmed the Conqueror), İstanbul: İstanbul University, the Institute of Medical History.